Battling Tornados

A Guide to Survival and Aid

Prepping and Survival Series

M. Usman

Mendon Cottage Books

JD-Biz Publishing

Our books are available at
1. Amazon
2. Barnes and Noble
3. Itunes
4. Kobo
5. Smashwords
6. Google Play Books

Table of Contents

Preface

Tornados are a havoc creating, damage wrecking, and windy revenge of nature on earth. Escaping the wrath of the tornado is no easy task. However, we simply cannot give up on our survival and hence we plan and work out our strategies to combat it.

In this book we will try to start off by explaining to you how these devilish things are created and show you some of their signs. We will then show you how the system has been established to provide you with watches and warnings and stress upon the importance of planning. Surely we will give you plans and various tips on how to face the tornado and we sum it all up by giving you the disaster kits and the supplies you require. Lastly, we will give you an insight into a crucial element which is the first aid treatment for the basic wounds that you might suffer from.

Chapter 1 – Introduction

Tornados are one of the most dreaded natural disasters. Oblivious to anything along the path, it mercilessly destroys everything and everyone without giving a moment's notice. They do not have a fixed time for occurrences, but there frequency of appearances increases in the spring and summer. They are most expected between 3 pm to 9 pm. However, there are no limitations to time, date, and locations. If the tornado gets its conditions, it will appear. Unlike floods, where the areas prone to that particular disaster can be marked, the tornados are more of a surprise visitor. In the United States of America, over one thousand tornados are reported annually and they have not yet been able to mark all possible localities where they can occur. As the technology is getting better, even more areas are now being added to the constant watches and warning systems. Moreover, these systems are being upgraded for more timely information to aid survival.

How are these havoc creating monsters born?

A giant air ball, a huge column of rotating column of air, etc. are the most acceptable depictions of a tornado. It lowers from the heavens and brings the thunderstorm to the earth. The most deadly of their kinds, have rotating winds of as high as two hundred and fifty miles per hour. Imagine what this can do? This giant speeding angry wind formation can uproot trees and demolish any well-constructed building. What's even more dangerous is that they can turn all these things as fatal missiles and hurl them towards the people and other places to create even more destructions.

Their sizes may vary and so can their strengths, ranging from a few yards wide, briefly touching the ground, to being miles wide and sometimes traveling more than fifty miles! They can confirm your deepest nightmares. These gigantic tornados, although thankfully, only account for two percent of the total tornado occurrences, but they account for seventy percent of the total casualties.

The breeding conditions for tornados are the severe thunderstorms that occur in warmer unstable and moist air and they head along the colder fronts. These thunderstorms also are the cause for massive hailstorms and colossal winds. The storms occurring in spring time create the perfect conditions, area wise, for these storms to occur.

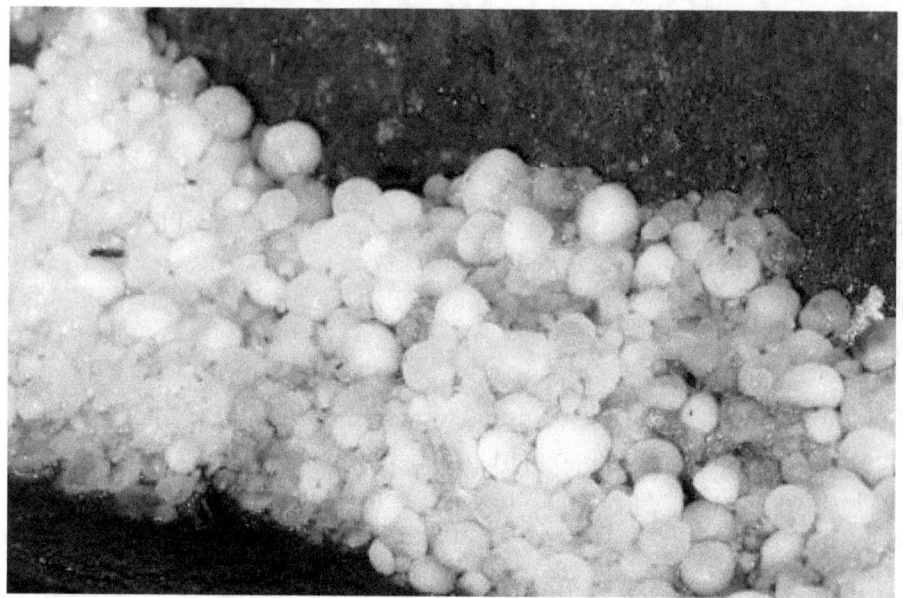

Hurricanes and tropical storms can also become a cause for the creation of tornados. These are more common to the center of the storm path, or to its right side, when the storm arrives ashore. The famous hurricane of Beulah in 1967 produced one hundred and forty eight tornados in the south of Texas.

Even though we agree that the tornados are wildly damaging, still this catastrophe can be minimized if we take precautions beforehand. Timely information is priceless in any disaster situation. Both lives and damages to properties can be reduced. A battery operated radio can increase your survival chances. You should also keep in touch with your local national weather service office for all updated information regarding the building of storms in your locality.

Chapter 2 - The Aid of Awareness

You should be able to differentiate between the watches and warnings put out by the national weather system. Mixing these two up can be playing with your life. A **watch** indicates that the conditions are building up that favor a tornado. It does not mean that a tornado is coming your way, but it indicates that the likelihood that you might be facing one soon is increasing. For instance, a watch given out for a severe thunderstorm means that you may expect it in approximately the next six hours. This is within an area covering 120 miles wide to 400 miles long. The purpose of a watch is to warn you in advance so that you can do all in your power to escape or prepare for a storm or a tornado, in advance, and be in a better position to fight it.

A **warning,** on the other hand, means that the planning period is over. You have approximately thirty minutes of time before the disaster strikes you. The national weather service issues a warning on a county to county basis. This is basically the last signal to be prepared.

Do not be lured into a false sense of security. If you do not see a tornado making its way towards you, that does not mean you are safe. They are usually transparent until they pick up their ammunitions, which are the dust and debris. So, stay alert and on your toes if you are witnessing high speed winds.

Check outside to see if it's not raining. Well if it isn't, that's a bad sign because tornados occur in conditions that are NOT rainy. This rule is especially for all the semiarid conditions. They are associated with a strong updraft of wind, so rain does not appear next to a tornado. However, a very large size of hail is an indication of a tornado. In areas that are humid, rain may wrap itself around the tornado making it difficult to spot.

Waterspouts are basically a weaker form of a tornado. These are most common in the regions of the gulf coast and the southeastern states of the United States of America. In the western part of the USA these waterspouts occur in late winter season. These tornados are basically over a body of water and they occasionally move inland creating damages along their path.

The entering points for the winds have to be blocked. Inside of a house is normally damaged when these winds find an entry hole. This is most commonly found through the windows or any cracks in the roof. Keep windows and shutters closed. All that debris can cause them to break open so stay away from all such entry points of the house.

It was primarily advised that the in case of a tornado you should seek shelter at the southwest corner of your house. Though, this is not something that can be relied upon for total safety. Historical evidence suggests to us that any corner of the house provides us with the same amount of coverage from the tornado.

What to do then? The solution in these circumstances is to basically seek a place in the lowest portion of the house, as far away from the windows as possible. A smaller room or a closet should be given preference. The places near the corners and windows are certainly not safe, because of the damaging debris the tornado can bring forth with it.

There are myths that have been passed on from generations that in the situation of a tornado you should open the windows of the house, because the differences between the air pressures inside and outside of the house can cause it to explode. This is NOT true. The air pressure differences are not strong enough to damage the house. Houses get damaged by the violent winds. These winds combined with the heavy debris they carry become the factor that damages the houses.

It was also suggested by people from past times and folklore that in the event that you get caught up in a tornado situation while driving, you should drive at right angles. Please do NOT depend on the assumption that tornados travel in a straight line. The curvature of the roads may lead you closer to its angle. Apart from that, so many things may go wrong; you may not be able to get a complete idea of the direction of the storm. In the stormy conditions it may also happen that the tornado in front of you is not the only tornado. There might be several tornados that may simply be blocked from your vision because of the poor visibility caused by the winds and the debris.

So what should you do then? The answer is simple, even though making sure you follow it according to your situation may be not that easy. Turn away from the tornado and move towards a more sturdy building and move to the lowest level in the vicinity. If there is no building close by, abort your vehicle, and lay down on the lowest portion of the road that you can find. Make sure that the particular portion of the road is not flooded. Cover your head and neck very carefully. NEVER make the mistake of finding refuge under an underpass or a bridge.

Chapter 3 - Plan for a Tornado

A safety plan is the key in every disastrous situation, and we cannot stress on its importance to make you realize that this could be the difference between your life and death.

Develop a family disaster plan as soon as you move into your house. The planning procedure should consist of the following key things:

- Learn about the exposure or risk of the tornados in your area. Don't be fooled if the area in which you reside has never witnessed a tornado. Okay, I agree that your risk is low, and some areas may experience a higher risk, but in the events of nature nothing can be an absolute certainly. You will be better off being prepared for an event than being caught up by a surprise.

- Choose and establish a safe hiding spot for your entire family. As we just told you, the lowest possible location of the house, typically the basement, is the safest place in the scenario of a tornado. A basement is an ideal location because of the absence of windows, which are very threatening in the case of a tornado. If your house does not have a basement, utilize an interior hallway or any room on the lowest possible floor. Having the protection of extra walls between you and the exterior of the house will provide you with an extra layer of insulation from the debris. Avoid picking a safe location with the presence of windows or glass doors and your survival chances will increase, as there are only two percent of tornados that can damage an entire building.

If your area is prone to the unfortunate events of tornados it will be a wise decision to reinforce your selected hiding place and provide it with some extra protection. This will allow you to build a safe room where you can take your supplies and seek refuge.

If you are currently in a high rise premises, you may find that there is not enough time to reach a safe lower floor. Select a place in a passage at the center of the building. The center of the constructed premises is stronger than the other parts.

If you live in a mobile home structure, seek shelter in a close by, strong built, building as that mobile home is more prone to be damaged heavily by a tornado than a strongly built structure. You may seek shelter in your mobile home only if a designated area has been given to it while planning for tornados during its construction.

Discuss a warning plan for your community. Many localities have sirens for this purpose with a few members keeping watches. You may also use battery operated radios to keep in touch with the overall situation. If you are travelling, keep in touch with all the names of the counties that you have crossed and the ones in which you are travelling to keep informed about the direction of the storm.

Practice is what makes you perfect and believe me, you will get confused if you get stuck in a disaster situation. Therefore, it is very important that your family members get practice drills. These drills will reduce the panic on the given day and will keep your head clear. Make sure that the entire family participates.

Get in touch with the plans for emergency kept by the child's school and your work places. Also make sure you recognize all the safe locations that you are supposed to head toward and learn them. Please make sure practice drills take place in all such places.

Protecting your property

At the time of the storm your mind will naturally only go towards survival and you won't even give a second thought to the important items that need to be secured as well. Therefore, the best plan of action is to make a list of all such items beforehand.

Get your trees and plantation trimmed properly. This can prove to be a huge benefit for you in the situation of a tornado. You can make the trees more wind resistant by removing the dead branches. This will allow the wind to blow through them without tagging them along its path. Also, as soon as you see signs of an approaching storm, make sure that any debris that can be collected is indeed collected before the arrival of the tornado, as you don't want all these items hurled at you at high speeds.

If you reside in an area that is frequently visited by the dreaded tornados, kindly make sure that you insert shutters as a permanent solution in your windows. Also make sure that if there are any doors or cracks that need to be fixed, you repair them before they become something terrible for your memory.

Chapter 4 - First Aid Supplies

This section deals with all possible first aid and helpful materials for your kit. Remember not only medications are required, but it should also be kept in mind that there might be several helpful materials that will be of your aid in any survival scenarios.

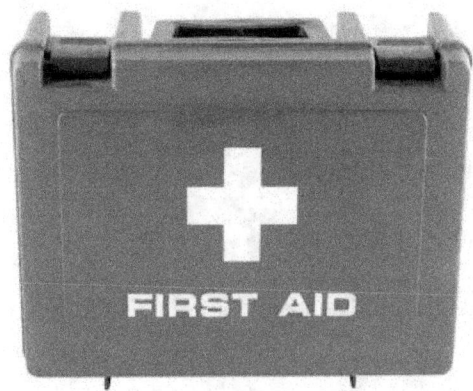

- Antibiotic ointment.

- Skin disinfectant spray.

- Eye drops.

- Spare prescriptions.

- Ear and nose drops.

- Children's aspirin.

- Benadryl.

- Diarrhea medication.

- Hydrogen peroxide.

- Cold/Cough medicine.

- Old pairs of eyeglasses.

- Insect repellent.

Drugs

- Antibiotic ointment.
- Hydrogen peroxide.
- Eye drops.
- Prescriptions.
- Diarrhea medicine.
- Aspirin and non-aspirin tablets.
- Wrapped alcohol swabs.

Dressings

- Bandage strips.
- Cotton-tipped swabs.
- Adhesive tape roll.
- Rolled gauze.
- Ace bandages.

Other First Aid Supplies

- Thermometer.
- First aid book.
- Safety pins.
- Scissors.
- Paper cups.

- Sunscreen.

- Sanitary napkins.

- Pocket knife.

- Needle and thread.

- Tissues.

- Tweezers.

- Small plastic bags.

- Instant cold packs for sprains.

- Bar soap.

- Splinting materials.

Survival Kit for Your Home

- Screwdriver.

- Axe, broom and a shovel.

- Ropes.

- Adjustable wrench.

- Pliers.

- Plastic sheeting and tape.

- Hammer.

Items for safety and comfort

- Tent.

- Candles

- Waterproof matches.

- Flashlight.

- Gloves.

- Garden hose.

- Blankets or sleeping bags.

- Portable radio.

- Strong shoes

- Change of clothing.

- Essential medications and eyeglasses.

- Fire extinguisher.

- Knife Food and water for pets.

- Toilet tissue.

- Cash.

Survival Kit for Your Automobile

- Change of clothes.

- Blankets.

- Jumper cables.

- Reflector.

- Flashlight.

- Toilet tissue.

- Gloves.

- Local maps.

- Fire extinguisher.

- Compass.

- Duct tape.

- Coins for telephone calls.

- Whistle for signaling.

- Bottled water.

- Paper and pencils.

- Battery-type flasher.

- Dried food.

- Prescription medicines.

- Light sticks.

- Battery-operated radio.

- Ropes.

- Small mirror for signaling.

- First aid kit and manual.

Survival Kit for Your Workplace

- Food, making sure that it is nonperishable.

- Flashlight.

- Pair of strong shoes.

- Battery-operated radio.

- Whistle or any other device use for signaling in distress.

- Fresh batteries.

- Jacket or sweatshirt.

- Small first aid kit.

- Blankets.

- Essential medications.

Chapter 5 - What to do in a Tornado?

Initially

➢ The radio is an excellent source for communication purposes and it will be your attachment to the outside world. Conditions however, may not be good for an ordinary radio because of the failure of certain utilities. Therefore, you should keep a NOAA Weather Radio, which will enable you to be attentive in the case for watches and warnings.

➢ If you are on any sort of trip for an extended period, keep in touch with the latest news updates on weather forecasts. This will enable you to take all necessary precautions beforehand.

➢ Watch for tornado indicators. Tornadoes strike quickly and not much prior notice can be given in their cases. However, if you can recognize certain clues the weather gives away, you may be able to figure and sense its presence.

➤ Dark and mostly a greenish tinge in the sky: Sometimes heavy hailstorm phenomenon may cause one or more clouds to turn greenish in color and this is your first sign of an approaching tornado.

➤ Wall cloud: Wall cloud is an isolated lowering of basically the lower or the base of a forming thunderstorm. It is even more suspicious if that particular wall cloud starts rotating.

➤ Large hail: Large hail is an indication that a tornado may appear. As tornados are basically spawned from huge thunderstorms, the chance of you getting one will increase if you witness an alarming hailstorm

➤ Cloud of debris: The funnel may not appear visible but a cloud of rotating debris is a safe bet of a tornado.

➤ Funnel cloud: Another sign is basically if you can see a rotating extension of the lower part of a cloud or its base.

➤ Roaring noise: Not a very clear sign but the sound associated with a tornado is basically that of a freight train.

➤ Tornadoes may appear at the edge of a thunderstorm. Two incidents have been observed; one is where you can see a clear sky behind it and in the other the rain obscures it from your line of sight.

What to Do During a Tornado WATCH

• Keep tuned in to the radio so that you can get the specific alerts for your vicinity. This is a time that you can utilize radios to your aid. Tornados can change their directions and intensities, so updated information is the key.

• The signs that we warned you in the previous sections should be noted and observed and you should carefully plan all your activities, as well as, prepare and finalize all your disaster supply kits.

What to Do During a Tornado WARNING

• There is a great chance of electricity failure; hence a battery operated radio will give you more timely updates. We repeat that receiving constantly updated information about the approaching storm is very essential.

- Remember that the safe room that you planned should never have glass windows and more importantly reduce the number of light metal or plastic objects that can become a part of the tornado debris.

- If you are stuck and cannot go to your safe room, seek the shelter of a sturdy furniture table. This will keep you protected from most of the debris. Tightly hold on to it making sure that the furniture is really strong.

- Your head and neck are the most vulnerable positions of your body; therefore use one of your hands to protect them.

- Driving in a tornado is IMPOSSIBLE. Please abstain from doing so. The velocity is so much that your car will simply become a part of the debris. Walk away and leave your car, head toward a strong building or otherwise seek a low spot on the ground that is not filled with water.

- Wide span roofs provide you minimal coverage and are one of the most vulnerable areas. These include the cafeterias, shopping malls and auditoriums. So kindly avoid these places.

What to Do After a Tornado

- Even after the tornado is over that radio should remain your constant companion as it will bring to you all the relevant news of the damages inflicted and the roads and routes that have been blocked by the storm.

- If you are okay and your family is safe and unharmed check if there are neighbors that require your assistance. The children and the elderly people require all of our special attention since they are not in the best state to help their selves.

- Check if anyone is injured and offer them first aid assistance. Your community should combine and seek out people in need for assistance.

- The damage from the debris will be quite widespread. Check if there are any broken power lines or gas leakages. Report immediately in either case to get those supplies cut off to prevent any further damage.

- Only seek out people to help in your community. If you are not a trained expert, do not head out for disaster areas as your presence would be less beneficial and more of a hindrance for everyone.

- Keep your distance from damaged buildings. The havoc created by the tornado may be too much and may have made the premises very unstable. Even if your house is hit avoid it until it is cleared by the proper authorities.

- Use the following precautionary measures while entering any premises after being hit by a tornado:

  ➢ Wear strong shoes. Being cut on the feet is a very common source of injury.

  ➢ Keep battery powered flashlights as they will also prevent any fire hazards through gas leakages.

  ➢ Make sure that you observe the walls and floor to analyze if it is on the verge of collapsing or not.

  ➢ Fire hazards can be very common because of the gas leakages, so be very careful in that regard.

Chapter 6 - First Aid Provision

The damages to the mind may last longer, but that doesn't mean that the external damages have to prolong as well. We plan next, to guide you through some of the first aid treatments for the most common of injuries suffered in the incident of a tornado.

Bleeding wounds

One of the most common injuries faced by people in the occurrence of a tornado is a bleeding injury. The colossal debris can strike you in several places of the body and completely preventing yourself from getting hit would indeed be a miracle. However, the odds of getting cuts and scrapes are quite high. These injuries cannot be taken lightly, by any means at all, and instant first aid treatment is an absolute must. Severe blood loss may lead to the person becoming unconscious and the trauma will be heightened. Furthermore, open wounds are an attractive location for bacteria and viruses to attack your body, and trust me, catching any disease at that particular time is not something you would like.

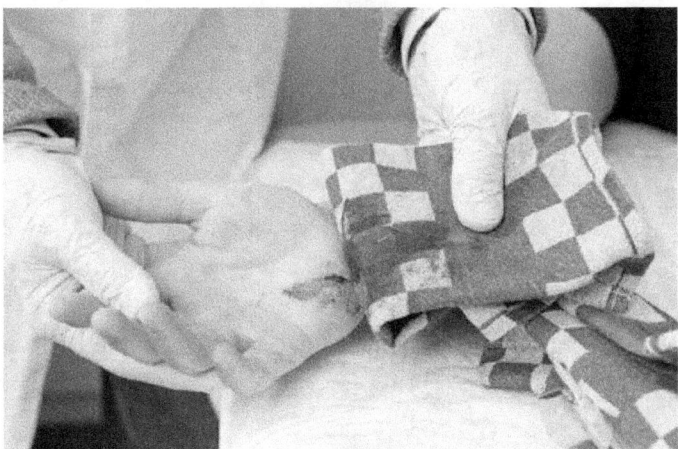

The following is how you can cope with external wounds:

- Locate the area of injury. If the the injury is on the head or neck then just apply pressure to the affected area and wait for help to come. Don't treat the wound with any chemical or put a banadage on, as you may worsen the wound.

- If the wound is external then clean it with spirit and apply a banadage to stop the bleeding.

- Don't try to close the wound on your own. Just cover it, apply pressure and wait for help to come.

Internal bleeding

This kind of bleeding is even more threatening, particularly because it cannot be spotted immediately. Having no physical appearance, these are really hard to catch and if they are neglected they may become a really serious condition. The following are some of the identifiable symptoms:

- The victim may become unconscious and if the internal bleeding is in the portion of the head, signs of paralysis may occur.

- Stomach getting inflamed and hard.

- Short windedness can also be a leading symptom.

In the scenario of internal bleeding call the emergency numbers immediately as there is little help that you can provide.

Burning

The incidences of gas leakages during a tornado are very high, as the damages inflicted on utilities occur commonly through the debris falling everywhere. The causes of fire being ignited are too high and therefore the number of cases which people bring forward of showing various burns are alarming.

Intensity level of a burn

There are several different levels of the body being burnt and these various levels are termed as degrees. The human body can be helped in recovery if the guidelines to the level of the burns have been figured out immediately.

Degree

The degree is a sign for showing the depths of the burnt marks on the victim. They range from minor to catastrophic damage to the body.

Degree Symptoms

The aching reddish skin is the sign for the first degree burn.

During the stage two or the second degree, the blisters start to form and the peeling of the skin initiates.

The whites mingle with the blue and the skin gets totally peeled off in the third degree. It is painless since the sensory system of the nerves gets damaged.

Fourth degree is an absolute tragedy. The skin and flesh do not survive and the bones are visible. Intense thirst and heat is felt by the victim.

Burn symptoms

➢ Painful when touched.

➢ Feeling very thirsty.

➢ Not bleeding.

➢ Bones can be seen.

➢ Peeling off skin.

➢ Red colored skin.

➢ Blistered skin.

➢ Feeling very hot.

➢ Stinging smell.

Principles of first aid against burns

- The first step is to prevent the burns from getting any deeper. The basic process to make that happen is to soak the wound in cold water. Avoid applying any ointment at random. If you have ointments specialized for burns then apply it generously. Otherwise, avoid applying anything.

- The open wound is an invitation for all kinds of infections; therefore you should cover it up with sterile cloth as soon as possible.

- Covering the wound is the preliminary step and it has to be followed up by applying proper bandages. In the case for burns the tightness is not necessary and merely the fact that the wound is covered is enough.

Broken bones

Types of broken bone wounds include:

- Fractured bone: The bone is broken but it is not fully apart.

- Closed broken bone: This is the case when a piece of broken bones is trapped inside the body.

- Open broken bone: The bone sticks out of the human skin in this category

Symptoms of broken bone wounds

- Swollen.

- Difference in the length of the extremities.

- Very painful when touched or moved.

- Breathing difficulties.

- Wounds on both head and neck.

- Change in form.

❖ Black and blue.

Treatment of broken bone wounds

No matter what happens, the part of the damaged bone has to rest and absolutely no movement must be made. This is the basic step for healing this wound. The movement of the bone inside can worsen the matter.

Next, you can use a helpful technique known as splint bandaging. What will basically happen in this technique is that two splints of wood and a cloth is used to bind the location of the fracture together. The fracture is then bound with ropes to make sure that the point of impact has been tightened. Next steps have to be performed by the professionals and first aid can be of little aid. All you need to make sure that the victim remains still.

Conclusion

Tornados, like any other natural disaster, can be combated with three things: preplanning, awareness, and proactive measure, with strict adherence to all plans. In the fight against nature you cannot panic and in order to do that you will have to be prepared. Being stubborn and reckless will yield no good results. Follow what we have told you and keep sure that you are aware of all the facts about where the locations and intensities of the tornados are. The moment you lose focus is the moment you lose the fight, and believe me you do not want to make this mistake. We are all helpless against this wrath of the nature, but we can and should do what we can in order to survive the storm.

Protect and guide your families through this turmoil. Keep all important documentations locked up in a strong safe and make sure you store that solid box in a safe location where it cannot become a part of the hurling debris. At the time of the disaster there will be no coordination amongst you if you haven't practiced the drills beforehand, so please make sure that you always are sure of what you are doing.

Author Bio

Muhammad Usman is a distinguished medical graduate of Allama Iqbal medical college (AIMC). He is a professional writer who has been in the field for more than 4 years. During this time he has produced 10,000+ articles, blogs and eBooks on various niches related to diseases, health, fitness, nutrition and well-being. He is a regular contributor to several journals related to medicine and surgery. He is the editor of several journals and newspapers.

Check out some of the other JD-Biz Publishing books

Gardening Series

Health Learning Series

Learn To Draw Series

How to Build and Plan Books

Entrepreneur Book Series

Our books are available at

1. Amazon.com

2. Barnes and Noble

3. Itunes

4. Kobo

5. Smashwords

6. Google Play Books

Publisher

JD-Biz Corp

P O Box 374

Mendon, Utah 84325

http://www.jd-biz.com/

Mendon Cottage Books

P O Box 374, Mendon Utah 84325